THE CHURCH
IN
NIGHTINGALE
SQUARE

THE CHURCH IN NIGHTINGALE SQUARE

A history of Holy Ghost RC
Church, Balham

Joanna Bogle

GRACEWING

First published in 2005

Gracewing
2 Southern Avenue, Leominster
Herefordshire HR6 0QF

ISBN 0 85244 635 7

Typeset by Action Publishing Technology Ltd,
Gloucester GL1 5SR

Printed in England by
Antony Rowe Ltd, Eastbourne BN23 6QT

A history of Holy Ghost RC Church, Balham

We think of Balham today as a busy part of South London, a station on the Northern Line of the underground, a noisy High Road, and a network of small streets lined with late Victorian houses. The sounds are of pop music and car engines, of buses and shops and crowds of people.

The Catholic church of the Holy Ghost, in a corner of Nightingale Square, a few minutes' walk from the tube, has a midweek air of being a quiet oasis. Not that it ever seems empty – people drop in regularly to pray, there are weekday Masses with a good attendance, and next door is a thriving primary school from which children pour in and out in a chattering stream daily in term time. But the building itself, facing on to the tree-lined square and flanked by sturdy three-storey houses with neat gardens, has an air of stability and calm, as if representative of something unchanging in an ever-changing world.

A look at the history of the parish allows us to turn back to an utterly different Balham – a place of fields and farms. This was a rural area for centuries, and for much of that time a full day's journey from London. When this church was first planned, this pleasant residential square had not long been built and stood on virgin soil, where only meadows and trees had ever stood before.

1

Of course people have lived in Balham since before recorded history. And for many hundreds of years, people in Balham have been Christian, and attended church regularly. But from the sixteenth century onwards, such church attendance changed. The Catholic Mass was outlawed. Those who wanted to remain members of the Catholic Church, in union with Rome, owing allegiance as their ancestors had done to the successor of St Peter, could not do so openly. This remained the case for more than three centuries.

A letter quoted in the parish archives of Holy Ghost church, from a Mr Hale Saunders, says, 'When I came to Balham in the year 1870 there was not only no [Catholic] church but no Catholics except my own family and one poor old aged man and his wife living in Tooting. In those days we had to walk into Clapham to Mass on Sundays and relied for all our spiritual help from the Redemptorist Fathers.'

It was those same Redemptorist Fathers – running a mission that was to become the notable church of St Mary's, on Clapham Common – who were responsible for re-establishing Catholic life in Balham in the nineteenth century. Their Clapham work began in 1847, and by the 1880s it was clear that something was needed in the wide district of Balham and Tooting. By this time the Catholic Hierarchy of Bishops had been re-established in England and Wales, and church building and the opening of schools and missions was going on apace.

It was also a time of rapid social change. The railway had arrived. Balham station opened in 1856 and connected the district directly with central London, with trains running into the terminal named after the Queen, Victoria. What had been a rural district was rapidly becoming suburbanized as builders erected streets of houses from which people could travel swiftly to London for work. Among these people, there were growing numbers of Catholics. The religious map of Britain was changing: there were Catholic missionaries preaching, Catholic Irish

2

people settling in England following famine in their own country, and people moving into new urban centres as industrialization took hold.

With the appointment of a full hierarchy of Catholic Bishops in England and Wales in 1853, activity grew apace. By the 1880s, the Bishop of Southwark was Bishop John Butt. He charged the parish priest of Anerley, in South East London, Father Augustus Bethell, with the task of raising money for badly-needed churches in South London. A leaflet produced in the 1880s by Father Bethell, put Balham's case. Written from his address in Genoa Road, Anerley, and under the headline 'FIVE MILES OF LONDON SUBURBS WITHOUT A MISSION' his letter formally implored:

Dear Sir

May I beg of you a small contribution towards the foundation of a new Mission, for which I am charged by the Bishop of Southwark to solicit the help of the faithful?

A Mission has for a long time been very urgently required at BALHAM there being no Catholic church in the neighbourhood, though it is scarcely out of London, and quite overgrown with bricks-and-mortar, but a stretch of no less than five miles without one.

The price of land being very high, a considerable sum must be collected before the Mission can be fairly started, but as there is no more certain way of saving souls than the establishment of a new Mission where it is so greatly needed, there can be no greater charity, and we may be quite sure that the work is specially pleasing to the Sacred Heart of Our Lord Who will not fail to reward abundantly all who assist in it. Indeed S. Augustine tells us that if we save but one soul we secure the salvation of our own.

Trusting to your charity to send a little help to me or to the Rt Rev Bishop Butt for this very necessary work, which is to be dedicated to S. Joseph and S. Francis of Assisi.

I remain
Yours sincerely in Christ
Augustus Ph. Bethell.

PS A Mass is offered once a week for benefactors and their intentions.

This fund-raising went on through the 1880s, and it seems that some £200 was collected. But if anyone gave because they felt a particular devotion to St Joseph or St Francis, and felt glad because the church was to bear the name of these saints, they were to be disappointed, because the church that finally arose was of course dedicated to the Holy Ghost. It is not known why these saints were first chosen, or why they were abandoned.

Meanwhile, some French nuns, of La Retraite, based in Angers, were keen to do some work in Britain. With the support and encouragement of Bishop Butt, they acquired a building in Balham in 1880. This was a house called 'The Willows' and stood in Balham High Road, near where Du Cane Court now stands, opposite what is now the Polish White Eagle Club. On 24 August 1880, the sisters arrived from France, and a priest from Clapham's Redemptorist community celebrated Mass for them.

The sisters did not remain long in 'The Willows' and two years later moved to 'Oakfield', a large house in Atkins Road. Mass was said regularly in the chapel they created in their convent there, and local Catholics were able to go there for Mass. This was the start of what was to be a long stay in South London, and the establishment of a large and thriving girls' school.

At the same time, some other nuns, the Sisters of Perpetual Adoration, a Belgian order, were also planning work in London. They already had a base in Manchester and now, after a short stay in temporary accommodation at Streatham Hill, invested in a plot of land in Balham. This was really the start of the Balham Mission, which was to become Holy Ghost parish. The land they acquired was two and a half acres, part of what was known locally as the Woodlands Estate, and was at the corner of a square of recently-built houses. The sisters had a new convent built from scratch on this site, and in 1890 they moved in. On 12 June of that year the building was formally blessed and opened by Bishop Butt.

The convent was a large three-storey building, over-looking the square – which by now had been officially named Nightingale Square and was home to a number of families. (The original plan had been for it to be named Mackay Square – perhaps the builder of the houses was named Mackay? – but for some reason this was changed.) Next to the nuns' convent was a good-sized piece of open land, which they also owned. It was here that eventually the church of the Holy Ghost would rise.

The sisters' chaplain, Père Joseph Simon, was, like them, French-speaking. Ordained in 1871, he was to give his full energies to his new task in his adopted country. As soon as the convent was fully built, the chapel was opened to local Catholics for Mass. The first public Mass was said there on 15 August 1890. For five years, from 1890 to 1895, Père Simon said Mass and heard confessions regularly for local Catholics. Their number grew steadily, and according to his records, there was a Mass attendance of 600 by the time he left. This is a remarkable achievement and must have involved a good deal of seeking out of Catholics among the people moving to the area. The 1891 Catholic Directory lists the Chapel of the Holy Ghost in The Convent, Nightingale Square, as having Mass at 8 a.m. and 11 a.m. every Sunday, with confessions in English and French daily. This was, of course, a time of great and rapid growth in the Catholic Church in Britain generally. By now the La Retraite nuns had their school well established in Atkins Road. There was a Catholic Cathedral serving

5

Southwark, and nationally there were Catholic publications and Catholic events. Central London now boasted a good number of Catholic churches and there was talk of building a big Cathedral in Westminster. During all his time at Balham, Père Simon was concerned about getting a proper church built, and was in contact with the Bishop about this. A letter, addressed in beautiful copperplate handwriting to 'The Right Rev Dr Butt, The Lord Bishop of Southwark', and written from 6 Temperley Road, Balham, which was evidently at that time the priest's house, says:

I desire to return your Lordship my most sincere thanks for the paternal interview you granted me today, and also acknowledge with gratitude the £100 you so willingly promised me towards the building fund for the new Church at Balham.

May I venture to remind your Lordship that Canon Bethell collected a sum of between £200 and £300 towards the same object eleven years ago, which I believe was handed to the Diocese. I therefore trust that you will have it in your power to make your ultimate gift to our new Mission somewhere about £350.

I know the Gentlemen of my Committee so well, that I feel justified in offering you their thanks for coming so promptly to our assistance.

I have the honour to be,
My Lord
Your Lordship's most obedient servant
J. Simon

The parish accounts for the 1890s show a careful and thrifty approach. Bench rents brought in useful sums for the church – a family could pay a quarterly sum (it mostly seems to have been seven shillings and sixpence per quarter) and have exclusive use of a pew for a set period. Although this seems a little unfair on people who could not afford such a fee – and who therefore had to sit at the back, where free pews were reserved for them – it did bring in money, and ensured that a good body of people were committed to the life of the parish. (Such 'pew rents' were to continue for some years, and are apparently still known in synagogues, although they have disappeared from Catholic churches.) People also donated for specific needs – in 1894 a Mr Thompson gave two shillings and sixpence towards a Sanctus bell, and there were regular gifts of £3 or more from Mrs Allender and Mrs Goddard for 'altar furniture'. Someone was evidently employed to clean the church, and was given two shillings and sixpence a week. Altar wine and incense were, then as now, necessities, and there were other incidentals – a three shilling 'Christmas box' for the postman, coal for a concert (all heating was then done by open fires of course) and regular donations simply marked for 'the poor'. There were then in South London plenty of genuinely destitute families and no free health services or publicly-funded welfare.

It is not known whether Père Simon got the additional funds from the Bishop – but in any case the building fund grew, and the plans for the church went steadily ahead. In 1895 Père Simon was appointed chaplain to another convent in Hove, Sussex. He was to work there for six years, and died in 1901. The sisters must have been sorry to see him go from Balham, because he was a link with their Belgian past and, from then onwards all the priests in Nightingale Square were English.

Père Simon's replacement at Balham was Father James Warwick. With his arrival, the story of Holy Ghost parish really begins in earnest. His appointment, by Bishop Butt, took place on 13 October 1895. Just under a year later the foundation stone of the new church would be laid, on land donated by the nuns immediately adjacent to their convent.

Now fund-raising took on an urgent tone. One generous benefactor was a Mr Cramer, who lived at 'Fernside' in

Nightingale Lane. His large house still stands and is now (2005) a Jewish old people's home. There were also concerts to raise money, and modest donations from various individuals from time to time – a Lady Huntingtower gave £3, while a collection at the door of the church one Sunday in May 1895 raised fourteen shillings and sixpence. The concert itself involved expenditure, as a piano had to be hired (fifteen shillings), props acquired (seven shillings and sixpence) and tickets and handbills printed (eight shillings in all).

Using the convent chapel, the Catholic community was an active one. There were now a good number of established families, and for the First Communions in November 1895 a breakfast was given to the children (the parish accounts show that tea and sugar were bought for fivepence and fourpence each respectively, the baker was paid one shilling and eightpence, and 1½ lb of butter bought for one shilling and sevenpence). And although there was as yet no school building, evidently some sort of a school was run, as the parish records note prizes being presented for prompt attendance, and meals provided for the poorer children. Silver medals were also distributed on one occasion.

During this time, the clergy were living at 59 Kings Road, a house owned by a Mr Hart to whom rent was paid. But in December 1895 they moved into what is described as the 'new presbytery' – presumably a house nearer and more convenient for the new church, which was then rising steadily in Nightingale Square. This new presbytery was not the present one in Nightingale Square – which was not acquired until the 1920s – but another house nearby. In March, building work was done and work was carried out in the garden, including the planting of trees. It is interesting to note that the presbytery housed not only the clergy and a resident housekeeper, but also other staff, as parish accounts note payments to housemaids, and also items such as mirrors for servants' rooms.

On 20 June 1896 the Catholic weekly, *The Tablet*, announced, under the heading 'ECCLESIASTICAL EXHIBITION':

At the Convent of Perpetual Adoration, Nightingale-square, on Wednesday, there was an exhibition of vestments and church furniture. The exhibition was opened by Mgr Bourne, the Coadjutor Bishop of Southwark. In the evening his lordship laid the first stone of a new church which will be built at a cost of £3,000. Father Warwick preached at the laying of the stone.

This month also saw another landmark, as the parish was now formally registered for the solemnization of marriages according to the law, a fee being paid to the local authority of three pounds, two shillings and sixpence for this.

Fr Warwick – who was to remain at Balham for 13 years – was kept busy. He was assisted by a curate, Fr George Boniface. In addition to caring for the Catholics of Balham, they went to nearby Tooting to say Mass regularly. Eventually, there would be an independent parish there – named St Boniface (was this a tribute to the hard-working curate?). All this without, of course, transport of their own, and with limited funds and in the difficult conditions of a semi-rural and not well-off district.

The church was completed in the early weeks of 1897 and opened for Mass for the first time on 14 February of that year, with Bishop Francis Bourne again coming to officiate at the ceremonies. Parishioners had continued to donate gifts, a Mrs Clarke giving eight shillings for a tabernacle veil, and money being raised for lamps and other items.

The architect was Leonard Stokes, a Catholic, and son of a well-known convert, S. N. Stokes, who had been chairman of the Camden Society at Cambridge and obliged to resign when he joined the Catholic Church. Leonard Stokes became a successful architect, and the buildings he went on to design include a wing of Emmanuel College,

Cambridge, and a convent for some Anglican nuns in London Colney, now (2005) used by the Catholic diocese of Westminster as a conference centre.

Stokes' original design was for a classic Gothic church, with arched windows and a tower. It would have been an imposing structure in the corner of Nightingale Square. But the final result was more modest. The Bishop complained that the aisles were too narrow, and so forced a wider and more squat appearance, and the tower disappeared. More importantly, the nuns, after consultation with their Mother House in Belgium, insisted that their chapel be entirely separate, although alongside. They also commissioned their own architect to build it, who created a tall and narrow structure with slim Gothic windows. For practical reasons, it was connected to the church so that the nuns could attend Mass, the intervening wall being pierced by a series of grilled arches so that the sisters could sit in their own chapel, out of sight but still technically present at the Holy Sacrifice. Fr Warwick was not happy with the style of the convent chapel, and wanted it to be built to a design of Leonard Stokes' – which certainly would seem to have been more sensible – but at the last minute, when Stokes had already done much of the work, was overruled by the nuns' superior, writing from Belgium.

Leonard Stokes married an heiress and they lived in Balham, while he continued with his successful architectural career. Later the church was to acquire a porch, and a side chapel dedicated to Our Lady. This would later become the present St Joseph's chapel when the convent chapel was finally incorporated into the main body of the building and dedicated to Our Lady – but that was not to be for many years.

The church was named in honour of the Holy Ghost, as that had been the designation of the original chapel – by this time turned into a workroom – in the convent.

Next door a small school was built, also designed by Stokes. Fr Warwick did not think that many children would attend, but he was quite wrong. He had thought there might be twenty pupils, but more than twice that number – to be exact, forty-two – arrived on the opening day, 20 September 1897. The nuns from La Retraite took charge of the teaching and accepted responsibility for the school generally. The problem of space (the children needed a playground, and also room for the school to expand) was resolved with the acquisition of more land – Fr Warwick bought the rest of the corner of Nightingale Square for £250. This meant adding to the parish debt, but it was a case of building for the future.

At this time the parish boundaries were extremely wide. They had not been defined in the very first days of Masses at the convent – it was just a question of the Mass being available to anyone who could get there, and people travelled from quite far away to do so. Now that the parish itself formally existed, it included stretches of Clapham, Earlsfield, Battersea, and Tooting. By 1898 the Catholic Directory was listing Balham parish as having a number of Masses, and Fr Boniface had moved on and been replaced as curate by Fr Rudolph Bullesbach, ordained in 1891. Fr Warwick, who must have been a man of great energy and resourcefulness, was also responsible for getting Catholic missions going at Tooting Bec – where he bought an abandoned Methodist chapel which later became St Anselm's – and at Earlsfield. Quite soon Clapham Park was given a church of its own – St Bede's, built in 1903 on land given by Miss Francis Ellis in Thornton Road – and became an independent parish, to be followed fairly swiftly by the other districts. So Balham's boundaries shrank to more manageable proportions.

In 1908 Fr Warwick was transferred to another parish – Sutton, in Surrey. The parish was sorry to see him go and he was given a splendid party to thank him for all his work. He would continue with a distinguished career: after working at Sutton for two years he was appointed Rector of the English College in Spain. Later he was appointed parish priest at East Grinstead, and then retired to Felpham on the Sussex Coast, where he died in 1939.

His place at Balham was taken by Father John Moynihan. By now the parish was well established and had a life of its own. Parish notices for 1909 give something of the flavour:

Jan 10th 1909. The social club meets in the school pm Friday from 8 to 10.15. The young men of the parish are urged to join.

Jan 17th 1909. Fr Filmer will commence a mission for non-Catholics on Sunday, Jan. 31st. He asks you to pray earnestly for its success and to make it well known. [This was evidently a major undertaking: handbills were available at the church and door and people were urged to make the Mission known far and wide and to encourage their friends and relatives to attend the various talks.]

'Nov 14th 1909. Fr Rudolph, of the Capuchin Order, will give a lime-light lecture at the Balham Asembly Rooms on Tuesday on 'Life in a Monastery'.

A regular announcement is 'bench rents due' so this system was still running at that time.

By now, Balham had more and more the appearance of a bustling suburb. Regular buses to the City of London had started running in the 1890s, and fewer and fewer local people now had links with farming or the old rural way of life. But there was still a semi-rural feeling to the area – motorcars were of course only a new invention and few people in Balham possessed such a thing or could ever imagine themselves doing so. The little school was described by one inspector from the London County Council as being the 'prettiest in London'. Children played with their hoops in Nightingale Square without fear of traffic.

We can imagine the families arriving for Mass – the ladies in long dresses and large hats, the gentlemen in formal suits, the little girls in the frilled and ruffled dresses of the period and the boys in sailor outfits or Norfolk jackets with stiff white collars. Mass would have been in Latin, and said in a low voice, the congregation bent over prayer books. Talking in church was done, if at all, very softly or in a whisper. The atmosphere would have been one of dignified respect.

Outside there was a very active parish life, with regular Whist Drives to raise funds to pay off the debt on the church building, and other events such as concerts and lectures, usually held at the Balham Assembly Rooms Minor Hall. In those pre-television days, the church was an important focus of social life and local news and activity.

As the parish grew, so its place in the local community became accepted and established. The local weekly newspaper regularly chronicled parish events and activities. At Christmas, 1910 'Father Schofield, OFM, who was recently ordained at Bologna, sang his first Mass on Christmas Day, the preacher being the rector, Father J. F. Moynihan.' In early 1911 the Guild of the Blessed Sacrament was hearing a lecture from Mr E. F. Anstruther of the Catholic Truth Society on 'Some Aspects of the Catholic Revival'.

Every summer the children from the parish school had an outing, funded by members of the parish. For some of the poorer children, this would be the only occasion in the year when they left the confines of the local district and went off somewhere new for the day. This 'Annual School Excursion' was a major event and each year the parish priests asked the congregation to give generously to make it possible.

Pentecost was always celebrated in style. In 1912 there was a Solemn High Mass with a sermon by Dr Multerm of the Marist Fathers. In the afternoon the children had no catechism class but instead attended Benediction and then took part in a special ceremony in which they made offer-

13

ings of flowers to a statue of Our Lady. All of this cost extra money for the music, candles, etc, and the parish notices had a special plea: 'We ask you to give generously at the Offertory today to enable us to meet the extra expenses of keeping the Feast day.'

A major event was the Annual Garden Party. This took place on two successive days, usually in the garden of the home of a wealthy parishioner. Tickets were on sale for several weeks in advance. Funds raised went towards expanding the school, and reducing the debt on the church, which by 1912 was down to £700. That year, the Garden Party was held at 33 Nightingale Lane and seems to have been an outstanding success, as the debt was reduced still further. It must have been a very charming scene: everyone in their best summer clothes, some of the ladies with parasols, children in their big straw hats, and old-fashioned bunting trimming the home-made stalls and displays.

There were a number of families who took the lead in fund-raising and the organizing of events in the parish, among them the Carrigans of 91 Calbourne Road, who had two sons and were stalwarts of the parish.

There was plenty of activity at every level in the parish. In the winter a 'coal club' operated, raising funds to pay for heating for poorer families. Throughout the year there was a Mothers' Club at which young mothers could meet and socialize. During 1912 a Catholic Benefit Society was launched, which seems to have been an insurance club, from which, in return for a modest sum each week, members could obtain medical and other help in time of need. A branch of the St Vincent de Paul Society flourished.

The parish was also part of the wider London Catholic scene. A 'Catholic League of South London' met to discuss topics of social or political significance, and there was a Debating Society associated with the Guild of Our Lady of Ransom. Wider events also found their way into the parish notices – in April 1912 people were asked to pray for the souls of Catholics who had perished on the *Titanic*.

Above all, the parish had a strong sense of what the Catholic Church was really all about. During 1912 a Mission was preached, and people were strongly urged to bring non-Catholic friends. There was a strong message about the need for saving one's soul. The Mission involved attendance at evening services with special guest preachers, and a book stall operated: 'Mrs Kershaw has a supply of pious books and objects suitable for the time of mission.' Sunday Mass attendances were steadily rising, and the congregation was urged to attend weekday Mass and the various extra activities, such as the Children of Mary – who met on Sunday afternoons – and the processions and devotions in honour of the Blessed Sacrament.

There were weddings, too – in the summer of 1913 the local newspaper reported 'a wedding of considerable local interest was solemnised at the Church of the Holy Ghost, Nightingale Square, Balham' when Miss Ruby Hoban, daughter of Mr and Mrs J. Hoban of 76 Ramsden Road married Mr Frank Wallace Last, son of Lt and Mrs C. W. Last, RN, of 74 Ramsden Road. 'A large and fashionable congregation witnessed the ceremony, which was performed by Father Torrance.' Details of the wedding reception, complete with a list of guests, were published, together with a full list of all the wedding presents – pictures, engravings, candlesticks, cheques, vases, tea services. (It must have been rather unnerving for any guest whose gift seemed modest compared to those of others.)

In these years before the First World War, everything seems serene and happy in the parish: it is a scene of an English suburb at peace. In the early summer weeks of 1914 it must have seemed as though this would all go on for ever. The Garden Party that year was held on 21 June at 23 Grove Road, Clapham Park. The parish debt was down to £300. On 26 June the Rector announced that 'The School Children desire to thank all kind friends who enabled them to have their Annual Excursion on Wednesday last'. The sun was shining and the usual programme of Whist Drives and concerts was planned for the months ahead.

Then through July the tensions across Europe tightened and by August had exploded into war. Known at the time as the Great War, it has become known to history as the First World War. Few in the summer of 1914 can gave imagined what it was going to be like, or the sorrow that it would bring to families across Britain.

The First World War

The parish notices for Sunday 9 August 1914 contained the announcement: 'The Bishop has ordered that the Collects from the Mass "In Time of War" be added at Mass whenever the Rubrics permit, and that the Litany of the Saints be said or sung on Sunday Evenings.' And there was a notice for the children: 'By Order of the London County Council. The Elementary School will re-open on Wednesday next at nine o'clock.' This is almost a full month before the normal start of a school term in September and was evidently a special wartime measure.

The following weeks saw further wartime measures announced. On 16 August: 'Today after all the services, a Special Collection will be made for the Prince of Wales National Fund (see letter from the vicar-general). We feel sure that you will give with all generosity.'

That month saw not only the outbreak of war, but also the death of the Pope, and a special letter from the Bishop was read in all the parishes in Southwark.

By September, with Belgium invaded by Germany, everyone was caught up in the drama and patriotic feelings were running high. A notice for 13 September reads 'Cardinal Mercier, the Primate of Belgium, will assist at the High Mass at 10.30 this morning at S. George's Cathedral. The Bishop hopes that all who can will be present to show their sympathy.'

Belgian refugees were now arriving in England and

Balham was one of the parishes which took in a good number, especially as the Belgian nuns at the Convent adjoining the church were well-placed to help them. The parish notices began to include some in French, directed specifically at them. One reminded them that it was 'interdit d'assister au services dans les Eglises Protestants sur peine de peche grave' – evidently some Belgians had been attending services at Anglican churches, probably in response to well-intentioned invitations from local families to do so.

A major recruiting meeting was held locally, to urge young men to volunteer for the army. Fr Moynihan attended and was seated with other dignitaries on the platform to hear a guest speaker 'Dr Holland Rose, of Cambridge University, and formerly a resident of Balham' speak on 'The War: a presentation of the British case'.

The local paper featured a picture of a parishioner, 'Miss Florence Walter, of Balham, an English schoolgirl, who has succeeded in escaping from the Germans in Belgium' – presumably she was on holiday or studying in Belgium when the invasion took place and managed to get a passage home. The newspaper adopts a rather propagandist note – to be 'an English schoolgirl' escaping from the Germans suggests something rather more splendid than merely being a Balham teenager.

There was evidently a strong feeling among Catholics that they should take a special interest in the plight of Belgium, as they shared the Catholic faith with so many Belgians. The sisters at the convent announced that they were now running 'une petite ecole pour les enfants refugies Belges' every day from 10 a.m. to 11 a.m. and 3.30 to 4.30 p.m.

Church rules about fasting – which were strict in those days – were relaxed for the duration of the war. In formal language, it was announced at all Masses that 'in virtue of the Faculties granted by the Holy See, the Bishop dispenses all the faithful from the obligation to fast and abstain on the Wednesdays in Advent'.

17

In these early months of the war, the local mood, reflecting that of Britain generally, was one of enthusiasm and dedication. On 20 December it was announced that there was to be a lecture on 'Devastated Belgium' at Balham Assembly Rooms – tickets cost two shillings and funds raised would go to relief work in Brussels. But the sacrifices were to be large. Over the next four years, there were to be many deaths among boys from this parish who had loyally joined the Armed Forces to serve their country.

November, traditionally the month of prayer for the dead, was to see a special Mass in 1914 for those who had fallen in the war – and by 1915, 1916 and 1917, the names commemorated included rising numbers of local boys. On Sunday 5 November 1916 the parish notices included an announcement that 'Members of the Guild of the Blessed Sacrament are asked to offer their Holy Communion for Lt Ambrose Wilkinson and the 8 o'clock Mass is being offered at the special request of members for the repose of his soul.'

In November 1917 young Leo Carrigan, one of the two sons of a prominent family in the parish, was killed. He had been a pupil at the parish school, and had joined the army and risen to the rank of lieutenant. The parish notices for that week have a particularly sad note: 'Out of respect for the late Leut Leo Carrigan and his family it is the wish of the Rector that the Whist Drive be postponed to Wednesday week and he has no doubt that all would concur with him in this act of respect.' This reference to the Whist Drive alludes to the fact that Mr Carrigan was secretary to the parish's Committee of Entertainment, and had long been the organizer of these events. Today, almost one hundred years later, Leo Carrigan's name is still remembered, as it heads up a long alphabetical list carved into marble on the parish War Memorial in the church porch. These names on the memorial all appeared at some stage during the war among the 'lately dead' read aloud at Mass and remembered in people's prayers. One imagines the catch of breath as a familiar boy's name was read aloud, and the news sunk in that he had perished. In addition, there were boys who had attended the parish school but who had grown up and moved away – the school kept a list of all who were serving with the army. Leo Carrigan was one of three boys from the parish school to die in the war, the others being A. Clunan and D. Gallivan. Over sixty former pupils served in all – one of them, E. Bilham, gained the Military Cross and two, W. Reed and S. Longdon, the Distinguished Service Medal.

The war dominated life over these years. But there was still an annual Mission – in 1915 it was preached by Father Kevin McKewn CP from Passion Sunday to Palm Sunday – parishioners were urged to take posters and put them in their front windows. Charitable work for the poor went on: a concert in April 1915 raised money for Red Cross work at the Weir Hospital and people were urged to attend: 'The poor of the parish have received much help and still do from the Weir dispensary.' Scouting was now becoming popular and in April the Scoutmaster of the Balham Troop gave a lecture, which was followed by a Whist Drive in aid of funds. Other events were curtailed by the war. The annual Garden Party was not held throughout these years, and people simply made donations instead.

In the midst of all this, in August 1915 the parish celebrated its Silver Jubilee – twenty-five years since its foundation. Members of the Guild of the Blessed Sacrament presented a silver chalice to Fr Moynihan, which he said he would not regard as a personal gift but as always the property of the parish. There was a High Mass with a sermon by Father Francis Denman, principal of the Xaverian College at Clapham. The convent next door also celebrated its twenty-fifth anniversary with a special Mass, and its grounds were opened up for a splendid reception in which Fr Moynihan and Fr Clifton welcomed all the members of the parish. The local newspaper reported: ' It was a time of friendly meetings, of the renewing of old acquaintanceships, and the strengthening of parochial bonds. Tea and light refreshments were served and a most pleasant time was passed.' Mr Hale Saunders, one of the oldest residents 'who could recall a time when there was no Catholic service in Balham' was among the guests, along with a number of visiting clergy.

At the jubilee celebrations, it was announced that the parish was now free of debt, a remarkable achievement and due to the hard work of people organizing Whist Drives and the annual Garden Party and similar events.

The autumn saw a Red Cross sale locally, with funds going to the care of wounded soldiers. Miss Feeney, of Holy Ghost parish, ran a Catholic stall as a joint venture with St Anselm's parish. It raised a total of £8. 7s.

December 1915 saw a lecture, 'The War and the Catholic World', given by Mr Hilliard Atteridge in the parish schoolroom. The announcement said: 'Ladies admitted if accompanied by gentlemen' which seems rather hard – especially as so many gentlemen were not around in those war years. Why the assumption that ladies who attended alone or in groups were in some way unsuitable? Or was is that ladies with husbands or sons away at the war might become emotionally upset during impassioned speeches? Evidently this exclusion did not apply to all meetings, as the following spring Mgr Hinde lectured on 'The Evidence of the Roman Catacombs' and the announcement stated 'The whole congregation is invited, ladies included'.

In March 1916 Fr Moynihan was appointed to another parish. He had been at Balham since 1908 and was to be much missed. Under his guidance, the parish had grown and thrived, and was coping with the hardships of the war years. A Testimonial to him was arranged and held in the parish school. This was evidently to be a formal event with speeches, and the parish announcement carries a slightly severe note: 'NO CHILDREN admitted, if they come they will be sent home.'

Fr Moynihan's successor was Father Henry Aust-Laurence. He had begun his priestly work at Balham, being appointed curate in Fr Warwick's time at Holy

Ghost church in 1900, and had then gone on to work at St Gregory's, Earlsfield, and at Cobham in Surrey. Now he was to return as parish priest. It was a popular appointment as he was young and dedicated and already knew the area well. But sadly he was only at Balham for a short while. About a year after his appointment he became ill, and he died in April 1917 after some months of suffering. His death, which occurred on Good Friday, evidently caused great sorrow in the parish. There had been prayers for him during his illness and much concern about him. His funeral Mass on 11 April was a major event. His mother and sister led a packed congregation of mourners, Fr Moynihan returned to preach and pay tribute to him, and all the children from the parish school took part in a funeral procession.

Fr Laurence's replacement was Father William Thompson, who arrived in May. He was to be the parish priest of Balham for the rest of his working life, and to become a well-known local figure, involved in the lives of hundreds of local people. Ordained in 1894, he had earlier worked at St George's Cathedral, and at Vauxhall, Anerley, Dartford, Dover, and Kingston.

By the end of the First World War, both Balham as a suburb and the parish of the Holy Ghost as a Catholic community had changed. There was more motorized traffic, and a far greater sense of bustle and noise. Daily life had changed, and young people's attitudes had changed, as war work and social mobility made inroads into accepted social structures. The old semi-rural Balham had gone for ever.

Catholic parish life was in fact to benefit from many of the changes that had come about during the Great War – the greater acceptance of Catholicism among British people following the social mixing that war had brought and the noteworthy courage of Catholic chaplains in the army; the sense of deep spiritual questioning that had arisen as a result of the terrible losses endured by so many families;

the growth of the suburbs as wartime industrialization swept old rural remnants away. In November 1918 as the fighting ended, the parish notices suggest a mood of sorrow, of formal gratitude for the end of a great struggle, and a sense of wanting to look forward. A notice in early November 1918, as news spread of the final battles, states: 'If peace is proclaimed, Congregation is earnestly requested to come to the church for Evening Service to give thanks to Almighty God.'

Elsewhere in Europe, the war had ushered in an era of revolution, panic, and uncertainty that was to result in the rise of the Soviet Union and Nazi Germany with their attendant miseries, but in Britain, the victor's camp, there was a strong sense of hope that peaceful years now lay ahead. However, as the Armistice was announced in that Autumn of 1918 there were a good many families in the parish whose thoughts must have been with their dead sons who would never return, and whose young lives would in due course simply be summed up by the marble War Memorial which would be erected in the church, bearing their names. Even a century later, this simple monument has the power to move and stir the thoughts of the visitor: it is a comparatively long list for a small and recently-established community. The names on it belong to young men who never really knew the Balham that was to become known as a noisy and busy suburb – theirs was a quieter and very different collection of streets and houses, in an England where the pace of life was measured and everything seemed unchanging and secure: from there to the rattle of machine-gun fire and the massive onslaught of mechanized warfare must have been a savage journey.

The 1920s and 30s

The years immediately following the First World War were to be busy ones in the parish – it was a time of steady expansion as Balham was consolidated as a commuter suburb. The 'Lenten returns' for the year January to December 1920 (sent in at April 1921) gave an average Mass attendance of 662, with 50 baptisms of children and 12 conversions. Attendance at afternoon Benediction was 126 and in the evening 160. The returns asked for numbers of male and female communicants, and it is interesting that there are almost twice as many of the latter.

The congregation of the church in Nightingale Square grew: Catholic families moved to the district because they knew there was a church there that would serve their needs; there were converts; and there was also a strong sense of evangelistic zeal throughout the Catholic community in Britain during these years. There were groups and organizations dedicated to spreading knowledge of the Catholic faith and winning converts. There were talks and meetings, pamphlets and magazines all dedicated to this aim and a bustling suburb of London was very much affected by all of this. In November 1923 a special guest preacher, Father Norbert Jones, came to Balham and preached on 'St Francis of Sales' work for the conversion of Protestants'.

Catholics were acutely aware of their spiritual duties: Sunday Mass as a serious obligation and attendance at other services such as Benediction fairly often, regular confession of sins, and involvement in the increasing number of organizations dedicated to various aspects of church life. There was a vast range: the Guild of the Blessed Sacrament, the (still new and extremely popular) Scouts and Guides, catechism classes for children, fund-raising groups of all kinds, and organizations promoting the work of the foreign missions. Among the Sunday notices there was one which appeared with almost weekly regularity: people were urged to 'sanctify Sunday' by attending Benediction in the afternoon in addition to Mass in the morning.

There were some notable highlights. In December 1923 the Board of Education approved an extension to the parish school – evidently following a good deal of campaigning and correspondence on the part of the parish priest and others. This meant that public funds were to be used to add extra classrooms for what was now a fairly large establishment.

Some parish notices show how changes were occurring that would have seemed extraordinary a couple of decades earlier. On 9 November 1924 the notices state:

> This evening the Electric Light which has been lately installed will be used in the Church for the first time. Ask the people to come in full numbers in thanksgiving. Fr Thompson is making an appeal to members of the Congregation to bring a personal offering with them tonight in an envelope so that we may be able to pay off the bill at once – it is a bit larger than at first anticipated.

Probably there was a good crowd just to see how the church looked when fully illuminated inside. The installation of electricity had been a goal for some while – in June of the previous year a notice read out at all Masses said plaintively 'Only £12 has been received, out of £75 for Electric Light for the Church. More must be received before Father Thompson can undertake the work.'

This was an era when much was expected of Catholics. The parish notices are full of exhortations to attendance at various events – Sunday Mass was of course taken for granted as an obligation, but there were also evening services, processions, and Benediction and it was expected that these would be well attended. A notice in December 1924 about attendance at the Christmas Midnight Mass is intriguing: 'The Congregation are urged to offer up the Midnight Mass as a voluntary gift to Our Lord and not to count it as a Mass of Obligation but to come to another Mass, preferably the 11.00.' An interesting point here is that the parish priest is not saying that the Midnight Mass does not fulfil the obligation – in fact, then as now, it most certainly does – but carefully phrases the statement to make people feel a little uncomfortable about being merely content with midnight attendance.

In 1925 a Boys' Club was started in the parish, for youths up to the age of 18, and books were requested for a library. Most of the boys and young men attending would already have been working, as the standard school leaving age at this time was 14.

In those days before television – and indeed before radio, for most families – going to an event in the parish hall was considered a pleasant and cheerful way to spend an evening and it was not hard to get a good attendance at meetings, club gatherings, and activities of all kinds. On Sunday evenings, a procession of the Blessed Sacrament would often be held around the church, with members of the Guild of the Blessed Sacrament and the Children of Mary in full attendance. Meetings of these organizations would then be held afterwards. Each February, there was a procession in honour of Our Lady of Lourdes. In the summer, people from the parish went to St George's Cathedral, Southwark, to join in the annual outdoor Blessed Sacrament procession there, for the feast of Corpus Christi.

One loss during these years was that of the convent. In 1923, with funds low and a difficult economic situation across Europe, the sisters in the convent adjoining the church were forced to sell their property and return to Belgium. This was felt as a great loss as they had played a major part in local life, especially during the war years. The loss of a building, erected with Catholic funds for Catholic purposes, was also keenly felt. No other Catholic organization had the funds to buy it, so the former convent remained unoccupied for several years and finally in the 1930s was acquired by the BBC. Feelings about this ran high for many years, with a sense that it was somehow all wrong for the building to have passed from church hands.

There was also the question of the convent chapel. This had been erected right next to the church, with a dividing wall pierced by gaps so that the sisters could join in the Mass. It was now sealed off completely and was simply regarded as part of the whole disused convent property. Meanwhile, the church itself was really too small for its expanding congregation and needed to be widened. A solution was found with the addition of a further side aisle, the whole question of the former convent chapel being shelved for the time being. This side aisle would be a Lady Chapel (many years later, when the convent chapel was finally acquired and added to the church, it would become St Joseph's chapel).

In February 1926 a meeting was announced 'to consider the ways and means of having a successful Bazaar at end of year – the main idea being to try to put side aisle on to the Church as it is missing at present'. This was the beginning of a lengthy project. Fund-raising was a major – even dominant – part of parish life. The side chapel, together with a crypt and a sacristy, would finally be added to the church in 1931 and between then and 1926 lay many parish bazaars and other fund-raising activities.

A programme for the 1926 Bazaar survives and gives a picture of the Balham of those days. Priced at one shilling (five pence in today's currency, but at that time quite expensive for a bazaar programme), it carries advertisements from local shops: 'Keirle's Bakers, Pastrycooks, Confectioners, Caterers – Noted throughout London for our Gold Medal; Wedding, Christening and Birthday Cakes'; 'Electric Light is the best light for every home. The Electric Supply should also be used for HEATING, COOKING, CLEANING .... The County of London Electric Supply Company Limited'; 'Holdron, Balham, for Gramophones and Records. Hear all the latest records in comfort in our new Audition Room.' The stalls at the Bazaar itself included a Household Stall: 'House Linens, Glass, Crockery, and Enamel Ware. Small Articles useful in the Home and Kitchen' and a Men's Stall, run by the Guild of the Blessed Sacrament: 'Brushes for Clothes, Hair, etc, Handkerchiefs, Pyjamas. Shirts and Collars.' There was also a Flower Stall and Games and Amusements: 'Misses Winifred Howie, M. Tierney, Dorothy Underwood, and Florence Wood, Messrs R. Arthur, G. J. Glover, T.A. Robertson and A.V. Watson will elevate and amuse us.'

At the Refreshments Stall, it was possible to buy a pot of tea for threepence (less than a penny in today's currency), pastries for two and a half pence, sandwiches for three-pence and jellies and trifles for fourpence. A note in the programme urged: 'Visitors are earnestly requested not to have tea before they come, but to try the hospitality of the ladies at this stall.'

The Bazaar, at The Baths Hall in Elmfield Road, was held on three successive days in November. Its chief organizer was Captain J. E. Enright of Doyle Road. He must have been satisfied with the result, as it brought large sums into the parish coffers, enabling the major rebuilding works to go ahead. Meanwhile, other more modest additions to the church appeared from time to time. On Easter Sunday 1926 a new banner for the Guild of the Blessed Sacrament was presented and blessed, the parish notices stating 'The donor of this beautiful gift desires to remain anonymous'. A statue of St Thérèse, the 'Little Flower' was also donated at about this time. Devotion to this saint – one of whose sisters was at that time still alive, in her convent in France – had become very strong in the First World War and many churches were acquiring statues of her. The statue still stands in Holy Ghost church today.

The war years were receding in people's memories, although families of those who had died would arrange for annual Masses to be said in their memory, and Armistice Day each November 11th was observed with great solemnity, the nearest Sunday being a day for special prayers for the war dead.

Confirmation, performed by the Bishop of Southwark, Bishop Peter Amigo, was a major event, and children were deemed eligible for this sacrament from the age of seven upwards, rather than from the age of eleven or so as is now the case.

In addition to clubs and fund-raising events, there were outings: 'Next Sunday the Guild of the Blessed Sacrament have their annual outing to Bognor. The Charabanc will leave Nightingale Square at 9.45.'

The Church Extension Fund was gradually reaching its target, and a letter from Canon Thompson and the curate, Father Peter Dorman, in January 1930 appealed for one final big effort, as £2,080 had already been raised. Fr Dorman was not in the parish very long, as later that year he left for a new post at Aldershot – perhaps as an army chaplain?

The Annual Mission was still a great event. A handbill was prepared which was the same every year, only the dates and minor details being altered. The style and tone had remained essentially unchanged since before the war, but the scale was by now larger. Visiting preachers would arrive and remain in the parish for a week, with sermons on different themes on various days. There would be some special services for children, and always at least one occasion on which parishioners were urged to bring along non-Catholic friends to hear the claims of the Catholic Church. But the main aim was to get practising Catholics to think seriously about their lives, and especially about whether they would go to Heaven or Hell when they died. A mission was a time to return to confession, to repent of sin, and to be made to think rather uncomfortably about the most serious aspects of Catholic teaching. The Mission handbill carried a note saying that it should be displayed in a prominent place in the house. This was the era of 'hell fire sermons', with preaching dedicated to the subject of salvation. The handbill read:

What is a Mission?
A mission is an extraordinary grace – the time of a MISSION is the time of Mercy and Blessing. A MISSION is a message from Almighty God to His children, to put them in mind that there is 'but one thing necessary' and that 'one thing' is the Salvation of their Souls ... GOD

CALLS ME to the MISSION – what must I do? I must attend to it as well as I can – daily if possible – I must listen to all the instructions and sermons – I must prepare to return to God by making a good humble Confession – I must begin at once to pray that I may have the grace to break off directly habits of sin and tepidity, to make a good MISSION and save my soul.

During these years the round of the Church's seasons was of course always marked and noted, although in a different style from today. The First Sunday of Advent was marked, not with an Advent wreath or talk about preparing for Christmas, but with the statement that marriages could not be solemnized over the next four weeks. At that time, it was Church law that wedding could not take place during Lent or Advent, as a way of noting the penitential nature of the season and avoiding having a party atmosphere during that time.

As a result of what seem to have been heroic fundraising efforts, the additions to the church were completed and on 27 May 1931 there was a splendid ceremony at which they were blessed and declared open for use by Bishop Amigo. Later that year a set of Stations of the Cross was also added to the church and these were blessed by the parish priest – who was now Canon Thompson and not just Father Thompson – on 27 September. The church had now been formally consecrated – something that is not, by Church law, allowed until the building is free of debt. The consecration ceremony was performed on 17 May 1934, by Bishop Amigo.

These years – which later came to be called the 'inter-war years' because of the Second War breaking out in 1939 – being a member of a busy South London Catholic parish was something that was interesting and absorbing, offering not only a spiritual message but also a whole world-view and set of ideas. In many ways, Catholics lived as their neighbours did – in those years, most people regarded regular church attendance as fairly normal, and Britain was certainly felt to be a Christian country. Divorce was regarded as something rather terrible, and the Catholic Church was not alone in stating the impossibility of divorced people marrying new partners in church. Abortion was of course illegal, and unmentionable, as was homosexual activity. Pornography was not available in shops and swear-words or obscenities were banned from stage and screen. To be a Catholic was to be part of mainstream culture in many everyday ways – but in other specific ways Catholics were set apart. The use of Latin rather than English at Mass was a major factor, and the liturgy in those days was celebrated with the priest speaking in a low murmur not easily heard by the congregation – all making it feel very different from any non-Catholic service. Days of fasting and abstinence were also relevant – Church rule at that time was that all Fridays should be days of abstinence from meat, and 'eating fish on Friday' was something that defined Catholics.

One area where Catholics were beginning to find themselves taking an independent stand was on the subject of birth control. Although not discussed publicly – and certainly not available freely to anyone – forms of birth control were beginning to be accepted and promoted by local health authorities. In October 1936 the Catholic priests of the Balham deanery were concerned to learn that a 'Birth Control Clinic' was to be opened in South London, under the control of Wandsworth Borough Council. Canon Thompson wrote on behalf of the clergy to Alderman George Doland to oppose the scheme. After listing the various Catholic parishes represented by the clergy – Balham, Clapham, Earlsfield, Mitcham, Morden, Streatham, and so on – he stated: 'It was unanimously decided that I should as Dean and their representative write to protest against a Clinic for Birth Control not only from moral principles but also because we object to Ratepayers' money being used for such a purpose.' Alderman Doland's reply was measured: 'You are evidently misinformed as to my attitude on the question of birth control. (1) There is in my opinion no moral principle involved. The advice to be given at a clinic is to be confined to married women and then only on medical grounds. (2) I have no intention of advocating ratepayers' money being used beyond what is already being done by the Wandsworth Borough Council.'

The correspondence then continued with Canon Thompson attempting to summarize the Church's teaching on this subject: 'God is the author of life – parents are only instruments used by Him for bringing this life into the world and they have no right to prevent this life, but if they do they sin against the nature implanted by God in them. It is an offence against their country and fellow men for by it they are lowering the status of the country ... it is a question of morality.' But clearly there was no meeting of minds on this, and the clergy's protest seems to have come to nothing as the clinic went ahead as planned. It is interesting to note that some forty years later, the notion of restricting birth control to married couples would itself be abandoned by health authorities, and a policy of wide-spread distribution of contraceptives to teenagers would be implemented, with consequent tragic results in young people's lives.

But the Britain of the 1930s was still a place where certain subjects such as this, although discussed among some, were not part of mainstream life, where an older Christian-based moral code was still considered the norm. This was also the case with regard to everyday outward behaviour, dress and speech.

At that time, in churches of all denominations, certain formalities were always observed in church. No one spoke in a loud voice. Women always wore hats. 'Sunday best' was usual for church attendance and it would have seemed very odd for a man to appear in church without a jacket and tie. Catholics always addressed priests as 'Father' or 'Canon' followed by the surname – the more recent use of 'Father' coupled with a Christian name would have seemed odd and disrespectful. Similarly, friends and neighbours habitually used 'Mr' and 'Mrs' and only close friends and family members used Christian names or nicknames. For a child to have called an adult by a Christian name would have seemed extraordinary.

Catholics tended to take a common line on certain international issues. There was, in the Catholic community, a general sense of support for Franco in the Spanish Civil War that raged in the 1930s. There was a deep concern about Communism, and prayers for the conversion of Russia (then very much a communist state, imposing atheism forcibly on its people and condemning many to long-term imprisonment and death in labour-camps) took place at the end of every Mass.

Catholics in Balham tended to share with their friends and neighbours a generally royalist and patriotic feeling – during these years a sense of being grateful for living in Britain, under a popular monarchy and without any immediate sense of revolution or unrest, was strong. This would carry on into the Second World War and be a defining aspect of life during those years. Balham was not 'multicultural' during this period: immigration was virtually unknown and English would be the only language heard in local shops and streets and on buses. Although there was considerable pride in the idea that Britain had a worldwide empire that included all of India (and what we today call Pakistan and Bangladesh), and much of Africa, it did not really impinge on South London life. Few could possibly have imagined a time when large numbers of people from lands once ruled by Britain would come and settle permanently in these southern suburbs, and when saris and Islamic dress, Hindu festivals and Islamic worship, African traditions and West Indian music would be regarded as a normal part of Balham life.

When war broke out in September 1939 it did not initially bring the dramatic changes that might have been expected. The uncertainties of the European situation had been clear for some time – people were prepared for war

Church of the Holy Ghost, Nightingale Square, Balham.

An early photograph of the church, evidently taken before the convent was closed, as its chapel (to the right of the church) still has its cross. The building was later used for many years by the BBC.

Church of the Holy Ghost, Nightingale Square, Balham, S.W.12

This postcard was one of a set printed in the late 1940s – some of the railings are still missing, having been removed for their metal value during the war. Note the sealed-up window of the former convent chapel to the right of the church. The chapel was not acquired and added to the main part of the church until the 1960s.

The parish school grew steadily in the years before the First World War. Here, two different classes pose for formal photographs with a banner and statue of Our Lady. There was no formal school uniform in those days, but the children appear well-dressed – or perhaps they were wearing their best clothes for the photograph? Long hair and large ribbons seem to have been the norm for the girls. Note the boys' stiff Norfolk collars.

Father James V. Warwick, second rector of Balham, who served from 1895 to 1908.

Father John Moynihan, rector from 1908 to 1915.

NIGHTINGALE SQUARE
R.C. SCHOOL
BALHAM

ROLL OF SERVICE
OF MEMBERS OF STAFF
AND OLD PUPILS WITH
HIS MAJESTY'S FORCES
DURING THE GREAT WAR
1914 -1918.

The names of those who died are in red.

A Commemorative Book was printed after the First World War to honour Balham pupils who had served.

OFFICIAL OPENING OF SIDE AISLE,
Church of Holy Ghost, Balham, S.W.12.

The side aisle of the church was added in 1931.

Church of the Holy Ghost, Nightingale Square, Balham.

Souvenir of Consecration, May 17th, 1934,
by Right Rev. PETER AMIGO, Bishop of Southwark.

CATHOLICITY IN BALHAM.

1849. Mission of Clapham, which included Balham, was founded.
1887. Balham Parish founded — PÈRE SIMON, first Missionary Priest.
Mass said in Convent of Perpetual Adoration.
1895. Oct. 13th, Rev. JAMES V. WARWICK succeeded PÈRE SIMON — Right Rev. JOHN BUTT being Bishop of Southwark.
1896. Foundation stone of Church laid by Right Rev. FRANCIS BOURNE, Co-adjutor Bishop of Southwark, on June 17th, and church opened next year.
1897. Schools started in 1896, and opened Monday, September 20th, 1897.
1908. Rev. JOHN MOYNIHAN succeeded Father WARWICK.
1915. Rev. HENRY AUST-LAWRENCE succeeded Father MOYNIHAN.
1917. Rev. WILLIAM THOMPSON succeeded Father AUST-LAWRENCE.

Freehold of Presbytery Land paid, 1921. Schools extended, April 1922. Presbytery itself paid for, 1927. Side Aisle to Church added, 1931.

Church consecrated, May 17th, 1934,
by The Right Rev. PETER AMIGO, Bishop of Southwark,
The Very Rev. WILLIAM CANON THOMPSON being Parish Priest.

Special deckle-edged commemorative cards were printed and distributed to mark the church's consecration in 1934.

K.S.C. C.219 (BEC SCHEME)

South-West London Catholic Schools

SPORTS

WILL BE HELD AT

SANDY LANE, MITCHAM

(Tooting & Mitcham F.C. Ground)

ON

SATURDAY, JUNE 29th, 1935

Commence at 12 noon

The following Schools are competing for the

CHALLENGE SHIELD

St. Mary's, Clapham : Our Lady's, Tooting : Holy Ghost, Balham
Holy Family, Morden : St. Andrew's, Streatham
St. Thomas's, Wandsworth : SS. Peter & Paul, Mitcham
Catholic Schools, Norwood : St. Mary's, Wimbledon
Sacred Heart, Battersea : St. Joseph's, Kingston
Corpus Christi, Brixton : St. Mary's, Sutton and Carshalton

Races for Old Boys and Old Girls★ - Sideshows

★ Apply to Headmaster for details.

REFRESHMENTS AT POPULAR PRICES

Admission 6d.   ::   Children 3d.

Trains to Tooting Junction, thence Tram or Bus.
Bus routes : 88, 87, 77 } To the "Swan," Mitcham.
Tram route : 30
SCOUTS will act as guides to the Ground.

*Tickets may be obtained from Children of the above Schools, or
members of K.S.C. (Bec Council), Dames of St. Joan, or at Gate.*

Come and see Catholic Action 'In Action'

The Knights of St Columba sponsored this major local sporting event for
local Catholic schools in the 1930s.

Canon William Thompson, parish priest from 1917 to 1963.

An undated picture showing Canon Thompson posing with a formal group of leading parishioners – late 1930s? This is a studio picture and has the air of having been taken for some major occasion.

Church of the Holy Ghost

NIGHTINGALE SQUARE, BALHAM.

JUBILEE

OF

Rev. Fr. Wm. THOMPSON.

Many members of the Congregation having suggested that some recognition should be made of the above event, it has been decided to open a fund for the purpose of presenting a cheque to our Rector.

In order that each of his Parishioners may have an opportunity of contributing a subscription, Mr. Heyburn, of 67 Mayford Road, Balham, has been appointed Treasurer, to whom remittances by post should be sent.

Subscriptions may also be handed to the Ladies and Gentlemen whose names are given below. One or other of these will be in attendance after all the services on Sunday, December 28th, January 4th and 11th. The fund will close on the last mentioned date.

Mr. Aldridge	Mr. Dilger	Mr. Snell
Mr. Bird	Mr. Dupre	Mrs. Schofield
Mr. Bilham	Mr. Grosvenor	Mr. Wallack
Mr. Booth	Mr. Jameson	Mr. E. White
Mrs. Carozzi	Mr. Johnston	Mr. & Mrs. Wilkinson
Mr. Cox	Mr. Precha	Mr. & Mrs. Young
Mr. Delaunay		

Canon William Thompson's Golden Jubilee in 1944 was a major event in the life of the parish.

Children lining up for a Blessed Sacrament procession in Nightingale Square, some time in the 1930s.

A school group with Canon William Thompson in the 1930s. There was still no official school uniform, which seems to have been a post-war development.

May ceremonies honouring Our Lady have always been important in parish life. Here, in a 1970s picture, the girl chosen for the honour of crowning the statue of Mary poses with her attendants. The girls carry small posies of flowers, and the boy a cushion on which the crown will be carried.

Father Martin Bennet outside the church in the 1970s.

London Celebration of the Martyrdom of St.Oliver Plunkett
1681-1981

This great Celebration, and Renewal of the Faith, today, will be led by

Tomás Cardinal Ó Fiaich

who will be accompanied by

Cardinal Basil Hume, OSB, the Apostolic Delegate, Archbishop Bruno Heim, Archbishop Michael Bowen, together with Archbishop Winning, Bishop McCormack, Bishop Alexander, Bishop Mullins, Bishop Walmsley, Bishop Lennon; the Area Bishops of Westminster and Southwark, the Abbot of Downside, and many other national leaders of the Church, and dignitaries representing lay, civil, political and Government organisations.

1st JULY, 1981

Clapham Common South,
Nightingale Lane, London, SW12,
in the parish of Balham, the church of the Holy Ghost.

50p.

Programme for the great commemoration of St Oliver Plunkett, 1981.

The presbytery in Nightingale Square has changed little over the years.

A current picture of the sanctuary of the former convent chapel, incorporated into the main church.

St Joseph's altar, which stands to the left of the main altar.

and it had already been a reality for many of them twenty years earlier. It was assumed that this new war would bring bombing, and possibly gas attacks on whole cities. Children were to be evacuated to the countryside and of course young men and women were called up for war service, either in the armed forces or in factories. In a small suburban parish, wartime life swiftly took on an atmosphere and flavour of its own. Interestingly, however, despite physical danger and damage, and life amid bombing and the darkness of the 'blackout', the parish in the years 1939–1945 did not change as much, or as dramatically, as it was to do in later years with the massive social changes of the 1960s and 70s. The huge cultural change created by the advent of television, and of the laws relating to divorce, abortion, and pornography, linked to large-scale immigration and changes in everyday life created by technology and massive prosperity, would all make Balham very different in due course. But let us look first at these years of the Second World War.

The Second World War

In the days before the formal start of the war in the summer of 1939 – the German army invaded Poland on September 1st and Britain and her empire declared war against Germany on the 3rd – London children were being evacuated to the countryside. There had long been a fear that London and other major cities would come under air attack and be severely bombed. Children were gathered together through their schools and taken to major London railway stations from where they were sent to remote country districts. For many, this was a traumatic event and many families missed their children so much that they later arranged for them to return – especially as no bombing of London took place during the first months of the war. A total of 154 children and their teachers from the Holy Ghost parish school were evacuated to Eastbourne in

Sussex. It seems a strange destination – surely if there were to be an invasion, any place on the South Coast would have been a most dangerous place for children? However, a note sent back to Canon Thompson announced that they were 'all well and happy and are being thoroughly well cared for'; the infants were to attend St Philips in Whitley Road and the rest St Andrews School. Thanks were sent to the London County Council staff at St John's Hill, Battersea, and to the Town Clerk in Eastbourne 'for the excellent arrangements made for the comfort and welfare of the children'.

However, within a few months they were back. The headmistress, Miss Mary Rochford, wrote to Canon Thompson in January 1940 from her evacuation address in Arlington Road, Eastbourne:

> I am so glad I shall be able to get back to London and to look after the Balham children again in your school. I have received the enclosed letter from the Inspector-in-charge here authorising my return and now have only to fix up the date of departure with Miss Spark ... Miss Donovan , the organist(!!) has the Inspector's permission to return as well. Two of us have to leave on account of the numbers, The Inspector sent for Miss Spark to tell her this and as we had already applied, he agreed to Miss Spark too ... We shall hope to get the singing going between us and make use of many opportunities in that direction ... As regards travelling expenses. Thank you very much for thinking of them – but I shall get my fare refunded by the L.C.C. [London County Council – then the education authority for London] . With all best wishes from the children and kindest regards from the teachers and myself ...

This was to be a very different war in many respects from the one fought twenty years earlier. Instead of a rallying-call for volunteers to join the army, there was a systematic call-up procedure for all men and women of working age.

34

All had to register, and if they could not prove that their present job was of value to the war effort, or that they had health reasons for remaining where they were, they could be drafted into the army, navy, or air force or sent to work in one of the innumerable wartime factories producing weaponry. Later, there would be a whole range of other possibilities including the Women's Land Army.

In the late 1930s, a large number of families in Balham were employing maids or cooks. It was not a particularly harsh or difficult life doing the housework for a suburban family, but it was restricted in scope and wartime now offered new possibilities. Many girls volunteered enthusiastically for one of the new women's services – the Women's Royal Naval Service or Wrens was regarded as the smartest, but all became very fashionable. For young men, 'joining up' was a matter of course, and they responded eagerly – very soon the young men of Balham disappeared into uniform.

A large number of restrictions were now imposed on everyday life: a nationwide system of food rationing, compulsory 'blacking out' of windows so that no light shone through at night, and censorship of newspapers and publications. Letters from young men serving in the forces could also be censored and could not reveal where the young man and his unit were, or where they were going.

As all this was happening to a nation with ready memories of the earlier war, and a deeply patriotic spirit, it all struck a chord and the mood of a London suburb in these early months of World War was one of unity and dedication in a common cause. A wireless (radio) was now owned by most families, and listening to the news and to popular shows became a major part of life. Because of the blackout, the disappearance of young people into the forces, and the evacuation of children, normal parish life was soon very much disrupted. All sorts of plans for any future development were put on hold 'until after the war' and a number of youth groups and organizations suffered the same fate.

The parish of the Holy Ghost had another change at this

time, unconnected with the war. The popular curate Father Flynn was posted to Seaford in Sussex and his replacement was Father Egan, described in a letter from Bishop's House as 'A very excellent young priest ... ordained last June'. In correspondence, Canon Thompson agreed to the change, although reluctantly, and asked that the two young priests be allowed to overlap at Balham for a few days so that Fr Flynn could show Fr Egan around and introduce him to his work.

Early in 1940 Bishop Peter Amigo sent round a special letter to all priests in the Southwark diocese, asking them to report on the situation in their parishes.

Bishop's House. Southwark S.E.1. January 3rd 1940
AD CLERUM

Rev and dear Father

1. I am most anxious to get all particulars available about the effects of evacuation both in the evacuated and reception areas. Many of the priests, however, have not sent me any returns. I shall be very grateful if you will let me know as soon as possible:
    (a) The increase or decrease of income in the quarter September to December 1939, as compared with the corresponding quarter in 1938. Most of the evacuated areas must be suffering considerably;
    (b) How far have the 'black out' and other circumstances affected attendance at Mass and Benediction, and the number of Confessions and Communions. At a time when we need prayer most, and when unfortunately many cannot attend our Services, it is most important that we should urge the practice of family prayers in the home to bring down the blessing of God upon the Country;
    (c) What provision is being made for the religious education of our Catholic children in the recep-

tion areas and in the evacuation areas? If schools have been reopened, let me know under what conditions they are working. Are any of our children attending emergency schools? Have many children gone to non-Catholic schools in the reception areas?

2. Forty Hours Exposition – I shall not be issuing the list for 1940 Exposition. I fear that it will not be possible to have it in most churches. Let the parish priests do what they can to have Exposition of the Blessed Sacrament in their churches.

He went on to tackle other matters, noting that £500 had been collected by Catholic parishes for the Red Cross, a sum described by the Lord Mayor as 'truly magnificent'. Finally, there was a note about Holy Communion. At that time, international Church law decreed that all must fast – from food and even drinks of any kind – from midnight before receiving Communion at a morning Mass (there were no evening Masses). Now, wartime conditions allowed for some relaxation of this, although by modern standards the rule still seems extremely strict:

I have received from the Sacred Congregation of the Sacraments, in a Rescript dated 13th November 1939, special faculties to allow the sick in Hospitals and nurses on night duty in care of the sick to take liquid nourishment before receiving Holy Communion. Parish priests who have hospitals in their parishes should make application to me for this privilege. But I wish you to discourage applications in other cases, for they are becoming too numerous, and there is a danger of the privilege being abused, and of scandal being caused.

In its formal tone, and sense of dedication to small detail in the middle of a war, this document is very typical of both the Britain and the Church of its day. It certainly reads strangely today that nurses having a cup of tea on night duty should consider themselves barred from Holy Communion unless special permission had been sought from the local bishop. On the other hand this strict discipline had formed a Catholic community that was strong in its convictions and admired for this by outsiders. The concern about the possibility of children attending non-Catholic schools is also interesting: this reflects a worry that they might be subjected to anti-Catholic talks or materials under the guise of 'non-denominational Christianity'. In fact, the reverse seems to have been the case and denominational preferences were very much honoured, both in the case of evacuated children and in the armed forces, where chaplains were appointed and Catholics given every facility to attend Mass.

In May Bishop Amigo made a formal Visitation to Balham. Correspondence about this between Canon Thompson and Bishop's House went into some domestic detail – not a trivial matter as wartime restrictions were already beginning to be serious. One note suggested that supper at 7 p.m. would be convenient: 'I am sure that some meat would be greatly appreciated, but His Grace is always completely satisfied if he is provided with a bowl of soup.' This was followed by a further urgent note: 'I overlooked the fact that the Visitation is to take place on a Friday; His Grace abstains as usual on Fridays.' This refers to the Church rule, then in force, that all Catholics should abstain from meat on Fridays. Some dioceses relaxed this rule in wartime – but Southwark was evidently not one of them.

As the war in Europe took more dramatic paths with the fall of France, and the scene was set for the Battle of Britain which was to be fought over the skies above the London suburbs, Canon Thompson still inevitably was caught up in smaller concerns. The presence of the BBC next door, in the former convent, had long been a source of irritation but now with extra technology it presented practical problems too. It seems there was either some repair work, or some other external need for a noisy motor. In a letter of

August 1940 to a Mr Chapman, Canon Thompson wrote:

It is almost impossible to carry on the services of the Church because of the noise of the dynamo planted on the very walls of the sanctuary. I think this must be unheard of. You did give me your word when you came first that the noise would not go on after six in the morning. A few days ago I had a Requiem Mass and Funeral with the corpse present, and sent word round to you and the only answer I got was to make the noise louder. It was simply pitiable. If it continues I have nothing left to do but put the case to our Diocesan Solicitors, for I feel it is illegal to plant a Dynamo immediately by the sanctuary walls. Please forgive me for writing this letter, but the position is too distressing for words.

The situation was sorted out with a grovelling apology from the BBC – and fairly soon there were a great many other things to worry about, as after August 1940 the bombing raids on London began in earnest, preparatory to German plans for an invasion of Britain. Bombs, air-raid sirens, shelters, sleeping in underground stations, and the sound of the 'all clear' were swiftly to be part of life for all Londoners. Balham suffered as did so many other areas of the city and its suburbs. The worst tragedy locally occurred on the night of 16 October when Balham tube station, where large numbers of people had been sheltering, was hit. A water main was burst and in their terrified struggle to escape in the darkness and horror, many people were drowned. The underground station is in fact not far from the surface, and must have seemed a safe haven. Many families had 'Andersen shelters', issued by the public authorities, in their back gardens, and others had ordered privately-built shelters of various designs. But for anyone out on their own, or for people without adequate shelters at home, the station – conveniently situated at a major road junction and easily reached – must have been seen as a place of safety as soon as the sirens went. In the chaos and terror of the bombing raid, a total of 64 people lost their lives at Balham on that night – a plaque at the station today commemorates the tragedy. Other bombs fell in the area that night and subsequently. There were bombs – and later, flying bombs, the V1s, in many of the roads around Nightingale Square, especially the small network of suburban roads between the square and Balham High Road. Later, when the war was over, there was the question of rebuilding and of compensation. As the war progressed, more and more families were made homeless. This, together with the rationing of food and fuel, and the short supplies of all sorts of things such as household goods, or clothing, made life difficult and uncomfortable – and this is reflected in the notes of parish activities.

In early 1942 there were plans to remove the railings around the church property. The idea was that they would be collected together and melted down to provide weapons or aircraft. All over Britain, churches, parks, schools and farms received letters informing them that the railings were to be uprooted and would be taken away. Canon Thompson received a letter from Bishop's House: 'The Ministry are dealing with us in all cases of railings that they want to take. They have now scheduled yours. The only grounds for appeal are (a) intrinsic artistic or historic merit and/or (b) public safety. Am I to appeal, please? If not, pse let me know that I can say they make take them.'

Canon Thompson replied 'Dear Father Cahill – I rather think the railings ought to be left alone – on the grounds of public safety. The British Broadcasting Corporation which adjoins our property would be left exposed. They have done what they could to protect their property, but if my railings were taken away, it would leave an open gap for anyone to enter.'

Letters went back and forth – the Canon seems to have been rather reluctant to compromise – but eventually an agreement was reached in which some of the railings were removed and others kept. Whether any Balham railings later played a major part in the provision of aircraft parts is anyone's guess.

A further question was that of registration for employment. Miss Rose Drake, employed as a housekeeper at the presbytery, had to appear before a local panel for possible call-up to the forces: a doctor's note stated, however, that she had flat feet and was 'permanently unfit for any work of national importance', which meant that she could stay on at Holy Ghost. The business of staff at the presbytery had a further hiccup, however, with the sudden departure of one of the other maids, following an argument about eggs (no small matter with wartime rationing allocating just one egg per adult per month). The Canon seems to have overreacted somewhat at this domestic problem. A letter in the parish files begins

> God forgive you – your ungrateful treacherous action will come back on your own head one day. At least you might have given a month's notice and not leave at a moment's notice when I was in the Church saying Mass. You have chosen a most difficult time when we have our procession and Forty Hours to do this ungrateful unnecessary act. You cannot with impunity throw over obligations which you have performed for years. I am getting old now, but I cannot remember one act so ungrateful and so treacherous as yours ...

In fairness, it should perhaps be noted that in wartime things such as obtaining and cooking food – and heating the church and the house, taking messages, and arranging for the running of a busy parish with few modern facilities (the Canon does not even seem to have owned a typewriter) – were all difficult and the sudden departure of a key member, albeit a junior one, of the parish team, would have meant real inconveniences. There were no easily available snacks, no takeaway pizzas, and no one had

41

mobile phones, computers, or photocopiers – even the quite trivial aspects of running community events involved a good deal of work.

Meanwhile, out in the wider world, the focus of the war shifted, with fighting in Africa, and then with the involvement of Japan and America, the loss of the British stronghold at Singapore, and so on to the culmination of the invasion of mainland Europe in 1944 and the final months of fighting. In the London suburbs everyday life had settled into a wartime pattern in which news from young people fighting far away, fears for their safety, shortages of basic items, and continued worries about future bombing raids, formed a background to the daily realities of work and duty. The V1 bombs continued the damage to South London that had begun in the Blitz from 1940–41. One V1 fell on the land at the rear of the BBC, others in streets nearby. The church's stained-glass windows were destroyed, and other damage was done.

In 1942 attempts were made to form a 'Religion and Life' group, bringing together Christians from all the churches in the district in a common cause. The idea behind it seems to have been rather vague – simply that of making a common Christian witness in an increasingly troubled world. Despite the goodwill, it was not easy to get anything of this sort started at this time. A letter to Canon Thompson from Fr Cowderoy, at Bishop's House, states clearly:

> His Grace feels that we ought to proceed with the utmost caution in the matter of joining with non-Catholics at public meetings. However much their goodwill and sincerity, things are often said which are against Catholic teaching, and we have either to remain silent and appear to assent or else to speak out and thereby, unwillingly, give offence.
>
> As for any participation in prayer His Grace would never countenance it even when the prayer is started by a Catholic chairman.

The Archbishop hopes that you will be able to think of some tactful way of declining the invitation ...

Ecumenical relationships with other churches would have to wait for another era, and would then prove, although cordial, less fruitful than had perhaps been hoped in the matter of re-evangelizing the nation.

At the end of 1944, despite the disruption to parish life caused by the war, and the departure of so many young people overseas with the forces, plans were made to mark Canon Thompson's Golden Jubilee – fifty years of priesthood – in style. The war news was good – bombing raids were over now, and victory for Britain and her allies seemed virtually certain. There was a mood of looking forward to the future, and of being rather congratulatory about the immediate past. A Golden Jubilee in the parish would bring people together. A brochure was produced and a committee formed, under the chairmanship of Father Philip McGuiness, the curate. The vice-chairman was Mr B. Avery of Alderbrook Road, the treasurer Mr R. Fincham of Fernside Road, and the Hon Secretary Mr E. Frost of Gosberton Road. Miss M. Rochford of Holy Ghost school was also on the committee, along with Mr W. Bolt, Mrs E. White and Mr D. Donald. Funds were collected for a Testimonial.

One link which Canon Thompson particularly valued was with a Carmelite monastery at Hitchen in Hertfordshire, where one of the nuns, Sister Monica, was a former parishioner whom he had baptized as a baby. In his letter to the nuns, he wrote rather gleefully 'Two Bishops and over 50 priests are coming for my Jubilee Mass on Thursday at 11.30.'

The Jubilee was a great event, celebrated with a commemorative booklet and much publicity in the local newspaper. Warm tributes were paid to the Canon, who for all his fierceness and formality was evidently a much-loved and respected parish priest. In letters to various old clergy friends afterwards – signed 'Billy' – the Canon described the celebrations: 'The School Children gave a very nice performance in my honour and a gift of £30. Last night there was a tea party and social for the congregation and a jubilee gift of £400. I nearly had a fit and collapse – I could hardly believe it ... I hope my old chest will soon be alright – it plays tricks with me ... pray for me.'

With the war slowly coming to its end there was a sense of hope and relaxation – but life was going to be very uncomfortable for some while longer. In January Canon Thompson wrote to his coal suppliers from his bomb-damaged presbytery, where rain was coming through a badly leaking roof. The letter tells a tale of woe but is unconsciously amusing:

> I have waited patiently for some coals in answer to my letter of Jan 5th but so far none have arrived. I again make an appeal for some – my premises have been bombed out and I have used up the small amount you sent last November – formerly I was accustomed to get six tons from you for the winter alone. Would you kindly note my name and not send to Mrs Thompson as no such person exists, Again wishing you every good wish for the New Year ...

Rationing of food and fuel not only continued but became more severe. In April Canon Thompson wrote again 'As a very old customer I cannot understand why you have neglected to give me even the small amount of coal that I am entitled to. I wrote for my allowance in February and in March when I asked for the allowance I was told I could not have it because the month was over ...' His letter mentions a recent stay in hospital and gives a rather pathetic picture of sitting 'by a grate with no fire'. It was a plight he shared in common with many other Londoners as war and its aftermath caused havoc with normal supplies of everyday goods.

The problems with the roof of the presbytery were considerable and getting repairs done was not just a matter of contacting a building firm. Permits and letters and licences had to be obtained from the Ministry of Works and the local Borough Council in a way that seems extraordinary to the modern reader. Wartime regulations were continued with relish by bureaucrats and the extreme shortage of all sorts of basic materials meant an endless round of letters and frustration. Fr Cahill wrote to Canon Thompson from Bishop's House in Southwark at the end of what was evidently a complicated saga over building works: 'Why cannot the Town Hall put your presbytery right – failing everything else? The licence is bound to take time ...' Essential repair work was only finally achieved after much delay.

However, there was lightness too. 'To celebrate the end of the war there will be a social gathering of the congregation on next Sunday at School Hall after the Evening Service' said an announcement in June 1945. 'Make a point of coming and bring your music and a friend.'

In April the wartime nightly blackout had ended and a notice for 22 April reads: 'We ought to be thankful to Almighty God for letting us have light once again at night and for ending the Black Out on Monday – St George's Day.' May saw the celebration of 'Empire Youth Sunday' – Britain still ruled India and large tracts of Africa and links with dominions such as Australia and Canada had been strengthened by the war – with a Mass in the ruins of St George's Cathedral. The Cathedral had been destroyed by bombing and would in due course be rebuilt.

The post-war years

As the 1940s gave way to the 1950s the emphasis was still on post-war reconstruction and coping. Names for banns of marriage still included many young men who gave their military rank as a matter of course – National Service was in force and would continue for some years. The stained-glass windows in Holy Ghost church had been

45

completely destroyed in a bombing raid, and efforts were now being made to have them replaced. The school – now back safely after wartime evacuation – clearly needed to be expanded. But in many ways this was an unchanged Britain – socially and culturally the war had not really changed people very much, and the real changes were to come in the next decade, the 1960s. On 6 July 1947 the parish notices announced: 'Today has been fixed by the Hierarchy of England and Wales to be a day of universal prayer for the nation. We must pray and not be so materialistic. There will be Exposition of the Blessed Sacrament from last Mass until Evening Service. All must join in this day of prayer and come to the Evening Service and Procession at 6.30.' Numbers at Mass and other events were as high as ever. At Christmas 1948 there were Masses at 8 a.m., 9.15, 10.15, and 11.45 in addition to the Midnight Mass and Canon Thompson made a special plea for Christmas offerings to be generous.

In February 1951 the Canon still felt confident enough of the Church's message and influence to denounce a 'Carnival Dance' advertized on a handbill he found in the church porch. He wrote to the organizers, quoting the Archbishop: 'It is not with approval that we hear of various social occasions dinners and dances and such like amusements which are sometimes held during Lent, irrespective of the holy season of penance. It is an abuse which has increased during the last few years, and it is one which we wish seriously to correct.'

In the previous year, 1950, the church's East Window was finally restored to beauty with fresh stained glass, and in 1951 the West Window followed. Money for this came partly from the official War Damages Commission. Some more land was acquired to allow the expansion of the parish school. The Catholic influence locally was considerable – in addition to his other duties, Canon Thompson was chaplain at the South London hospital, a big women's hospital facing Clapham Common, where of the 90 staff some 40 were Catholic, including a large number of Irish nurses. He was emphatic that they should not attend any church services other than Catholic ones, went there regularly to celebrate Mass, and was involved in having a proper chapel constructed at the hospital. The authorities were extremely helpful about this, and the chapel, dedicated to St Anne, was built to Canon Thompson's specifications. With its completion in 1955, it became in effect an addition to the parish, serving the needs of medical staff, patients and local residents who found it convenient.

Canon Thompson was, to say the least, tactless when dealing with Christians of other denominations locally. In 1953, for the Coronation of the new young Queen, Elizabeth II, the local Anglican vicar, Revd P. M. Smith wrote a friendly note mentioning a special service arranged by local churches in the 'Balham Picture House'. He added that of course he knew that the Catholic church could not be involved, but simply wanted to let the Canon know that it was taking place. Here, surely, was an opportunity for a gracious reply reflecting on the fact that it was right that all should be praying for the Queen and the nation at this special time. But no – Canon Thompson wrote briskly: 'I am glad you are aware that of course we members of the Catholic Church could not attend your services. We have received instructions [about] what we have to do from lawful authority. We are having three days of prayer to be concluded by Holy Mass to be said or sung at 8pm on the eve of Coronation Day', and he enclosed a pamphlet from the Catholic Truth Society explaining in detail why Catholics did not attend non-Catholic services. While formally correct, this seems cold and unhelpful, and cannot have done much to dispel the idea that Catholics were in general uninterested in reaching out to the wider nation.

On the other hand, there was plenty of vigorous and necessary social and community witness at Holy Ghost parish. That same year, 1953, saw correspondence with the local Member of Parliament, begging him to join those speaking out against the persecution of the Church by the

47

new Communist authorities in Poland. There were regular prayers, too, for this, and with the Hungarian Uprising of 1956 a generous response to a call for practical assistance to the many refugees fleeing to the West from the invading Russians.

In 1956 Mary Rochford, who had been headmistress of the parish school for many years and seen it through the difficulties of wartime evacuation and return, retired. Her letter to Canon Thompson makes oddly moving reading:

> My dear Canon, I send the enclosed official notice to you. I am very sorry and sad to have to do this at last and you know I would not retire at all unless I felt unable to continue the work ... I have loved the school and all those connected with it and believe me it is a great grief to sever my long connection with it ... Now that I have taken the plunge I know that I could not face any special farewell with my many friends and what I would like would be the usual little teaparty with you and the teachers in my room – as we have celebrated so many times and which I will arrange in due course ...'

Miss Rochford had taught in the school for 43 years. The deputy head, Miss Donovan, was in due course appointed in her place and the 'village school' atmosphere was passed on to new generations of children.

From the 1950s onwards, for many years Holy Ghost parish produced a yearbook, with information about the parish, devotional articles, and, in the middle, a large sheet of blotting paper so that the whole thing could be opened out and used as a blotter – this was still an era of fountain pens. In 1956 with Canon Thompson as parish priest and Father Anthony Shannon as curate, the parish of Balham still had something of the feel of a pre-war suburb, as seen in the advertisements: 'Shailer's Boot and Shoe Repairs'; 'G. Lewis – High Class family butcher, orders delivered daily'; 'Smith and Sons, 54 Balham Hill, Birthday and Wedding Cakes a speciality'; 'A. and E.

Tailor and Sons Dairy and provisions, 3 Oldridge Road, Balham'.

The 1960s was to be the decade of massive change. In February 1963 Canon Thompson died, and an era ended. He was much mourned. So many families had known him in all the important moments of their lives: baptisms of babies, illness and times of worry, school events, First Communion and Confirmation, weddings and funerals. He had heard countless confessions and celebrated countless Masses for the people of Balham, distributed Holy Communion to thousands kneeling at the altar rails and preached and taught and exhorted from the pulpit. He had been a part of Balham's life from the time of the First World War. To many local people, he seemed a fixture, part of the very fabric of things.

The new parish priest was Father Martin Bennett. He must have felt as if he was stepping into a giant's shoes. His arrival was to coincide with another major development in the parish. The London County Council – at that time the local authority controlling inner-London areas including Balham and its surrounding districts – decided to buy the former convent building next to the church, which had been owned by the BBC for several years. While this was being negotiated, a clause in the original sales deed of 1933 – when the nuns had sold the building to the BBC – came to light. This clause stated that in any future sale, the Holy Ghost parish should be allowed to have first option on buying the chapel. The discovery of this caused considerable excitement in the parish and the diocese, and the decision was made to go ahead and buy this building, which had of course a long association with the church dating back to the very earliest days, and which was physically joined to it. The key to the chapel was formally handed over to the parish, this momentous event occurring on the Feast of the Sacred Heart in June, 1963 which was in fact the very day on which the first Mass had been celebrated on that spot 73 years earlier.

At last the dreams of Fr Warwick, who had been parish

priest when the convent chapel was first built, could be realized. He had never liked the fact that it was artificially separated from the church and that the original plans of the architect Leonard Stokes, designer of the main church, had been abandoned and a new architect appointed. Now at last, as logic demanded, it would form a side aisle of the church and the whole would present a pleasing face to this corner of Nightingale Square. Work immediately began on reordering the chapel and reconnecting it to the church. It was decided to name it in honour of Our Lady of the Visitation, and accordingly the former Lady Chapel was now dedicated to St Joseph.

The chapel's opening and blessing on 2 July – then the feast of the Visitation – 1964 was a festival day for the parish. Bishop Cyril Cowderoy, who by then had succeeded Bishop Peter Amigo as Bishop of Southwark, presided. With the addition of this whole new side-chapel, the church could now seat 550 in comfort, with a further 50 standing. With the general reorganization of the church, the baptistery and confessionals were now placed in this new chapel, and the whole interior was decorated. The following year, on 3 May 1965, the Bishop returned to make a formal consecration of a new altar in this Lady Chapel.

This was the last major change to the church fabric for some years, and Fr Bennett's arrival also ensured that the parish was to know, as it had with Canon Thompson, many years of dedicated service. There was always a curate working alongside: during the 1960s, after Fr Shannon came Fathers Geoffrey Dove, Patrick Best, Cyril Williams and Anthony Pyle.

The 1960s were to see massive social changes in Britain, and also in the Church. In the 1963 parish yearbook, everything speaks of an unchanging pattern of life, oblivious to the changes on the way. In a section on dress and etiquette in church, readers are told: 'Ladies, as everyone knows, are expected to wear some form of head covering in church (cf. 1 Cor. xi 5). Those who do not wear hats can satisfy ecclesiastical etiquette by wearing a handkerchief or mantilla or something similar.' It was also 'unseemly to appear in church wearing slacks or jeans even though these may be appropriately worn elsewhere'.

But a foretaste of things to come can be glimpsed in the next feature 'Preparations for the Second Vatican Council'. This great Council had been called by the new Pope, John XXIII, who by now had succeeded Pope Pius XII. After listing the various Commissions and describing the activity in Rome as plans for this momentous event in the life of the Church gathered pace, the Holy Ghost parish yearbook described the work of various of the Commissions. Under 'Sacred Liturgy' it says: 'Among the innumerable questions which could be discussed by this important commission, one of the most important is whether national communities should be given greater scope to express themselves in ways conformable to their own culture, with which is connected the use of the vernacular in the liturgy.' No one reading this could possibly have thought of the arrival of guitars, 'folk Masses', informal coffee-table Masses and the other liturgical changes which were to be part of life for all Catholics in Britain in the next decade and a half.

But this was a time when so many things were changing, locally and nationally. The arrival of television was beginning to make a dramatic impact on the way people lived – now evenings would be spent looking at this box in the living-room, and TV comedies, news comment and analysis, and above all soap operas, would gradually come to dominate people's culture. In Balham as elsewhere, supermarkets and chain-stores would slowly squeeze out many small local shops. Large numbers of immigrants from the West Indies and then later from Africa and the Indian sub-continent were starting to settle in South London, and new accents and languages, food and clothing and patterns of living were beginning to be seen. Pop music began to pound out its beat, although not yet piped into banks and shops. Forms of dress hitherto reserved for the beach or casual holiday times began to appear on suburban streets – slacks, teeshirts, and soon the ubiquitous denim jeans. At the start of the 1960s, most women in Balham would go shopping wearing dresses or skirts and even hats. Most men would wear jackets and ties as routine wear. Everyone would wear 'Sunday best' for Mass. By the end of the decade all that was to change.

The Second Vatican Council

In a Catholic parish, all of this paled into insignificance before the great changes brought about in the wake of the Second Vatican Council. Called essentially to celebrate and consolidate the life and work of the Church, it seemed at first to revolutionize it. Changes in the Liturgy, planned as modest adaptions, were carried out with a vigour and enthusiasm that swept all away – the optional use of the local vernacular language was swiftly assumed to mean the complete abandonment of Latin, old hymns were abandoned and Gregorian chant disappeared.

Not every parish was rocked to its foundations, and normal life went on, but something of the old certainties seemed to have vanished for ever. Ecumenism was in the air – perhaps the ruthless crushing of modest attempts at inter-church co-operation by Bishop Amigo in previous years had served only to make the prospect seem more alluring. An uncomfortable air of uncertainty hovered over Catholic education – Religious Education textbooks were abandoned and a vagueness was substituted, with the result that many children were left confused about fundamental truths of the Faith. On the wider scale, the TV featured debates with priests denouncing central Church teachings, especially on matters relating to marriage and family life, or highlighted dissident Church spokesmen who seemed to say that there were no absolute certainties any more.

All of this affected every parish, even a busy and thriving

one such as this in South London. However, it does seem that while the Church seemed to be going through a troubled and difficult time, ordinary faithful Catholics carried on going to Mass, following Christ and doing their best to serve Him – certainly through all these years the Holy Ghost parish went on busily as it had always done, and was spared the tragedies of some Catholic communities where division and disunity caused heartache.

The new liturgical arrangements did mean some adaptions to Holy Ghost church itself. In 1973 the parish yearbook announced:

> The Second Vatican Council directed many changes in liturgy and worship and in the structure of churches and their sanctuaries. Mass facing the people was greatly encouraged to enable the congregation to take a more active and intimate part in its celebration. In the spring of 1971 all three of our altars had to be considerably altered for this new form of Mass, and at the same time a badly needed stone floor was given both to the high altar sanctuary and also to the chapel of St Joseph. While this work was in progress our new organ was installed to replace the small instrument which the church had for so many years and which was now beyond repair.

The three new altars were consecrated by Archbishop Cowderoy on 7 December 1971. Relics of St Oliver Plunkett – of whom more later – were among those placed in the high altar.

For Fr Bennett, this link with St Oliver Plunkett was reflective of his own personal background in Ireland. Holy Ghost parish had always had a large number of Irish families, and like so many Catholic parishes in London it owed its very existence to the revival of the Catholic Faith in the nineteenth century – which had in part been brought about by the arrival in England of many Irish people driven out of their own land by famine in the 1840s. Fr

Bennett fostered a strong devotion to St Oliver Plunkett, a brave Irish martyr who died for the Faith in London in the seventeenth century. Although some relics of the martyr were placed in Holy Ghost church, the main part of them remained at Downside Abbey in Somerset, where the martyr had long been venerated. As the 1970s opened, Fr Bennett began to make plans for St Oliver to be honoured in Balham. A statue of the saint had already been donated to the church back in 1966. In 1975, on the day of the martyr's canonization in Rome by Pope Paul VI, a special Mass was celebrated in Balham. Fr Bennett was in Rome, so the Mass was celebrated by Father Richard Quinlan. To mark the fact that Balham was now a very mixed community, with people who originally came from countries as far apart at Poland, Ireland, Italy and Africa, readings and prayers were in different languages. There was a special prayer for immigrants, read by an African, Mrs Chinewondah – a sign of the new Balham of the 1970s. But some things were unchanging – along with new hymns such as 'All that I am' there were old favourites: 'Full in the panting heart of Rome' and 'Faith of our Fathers'.

This Mass was, however, merely a preamble. Plans were afoot for a massive event in 1981 to mark the anniversary of the martyr's death in 1681. This 'London Celebration of the Martyrdom of St Oliver Plunkett' was staged on Clapham Common on 1 July 1981 and was the biggest single event to date in the parish's history.

The London Celebration was two full years in the planning. The St Oliver Plunkett Tercentenary Committee had Fr Quinlan as its chairman, Mrs Daphne Reid as its secretary, and a large number of local priests as members, including Father W. O'Riordan, Dean of Wandsworth, and Father P. O'Flanagan, Dean of Lambeth.

On the great day itself, 1 July 1981, the highlight was to be an open-air Mass with the relics of St Oliver Plunkett, which would then be returned – by helicopter, no less – to their resting-place at Downside Abbey. The Common was packed with a vast crowd. The Apostolic Delegate – the official 'Ambassador' from the Holy See to Britain – was present. Two cardinals attended – Cardinal Thomas O'Fiaich of Ireland, and Cardinal Basil Hume of Westminster. The event was hosted by Archbishop Michael Bowen, Southwark's Archbishop (who had replaced Archbishop Cowderoy on the latter's death some years earlier), accompanied by his auxiliaries Rt Rev Howard Tripp, Rt Rev Charles Henderson, and Rt Rev John Jukes. Distinguished guests included a number of Catholic bishops, the Abbot of Downside Rt Rev John Roberts, abbots from other Benedictine communities across Britain, representatives of Parliament and local government, ecumenical representatives from the other main Christian denominations, people from St Oliver's parish in Belfast and from another parish named after him in Warrington, and of course people from every parish in South London and further afield. There was an Irish Pipe Band, and as the helicopter took off, everyone joined in a hymn specially composed for the canonization some years earlier: 'Come glorious Martyr rise/Into the golden skies/Beyond the sun! Wide, wide you portals fling/Ye martyrs hosts, O sing/To greet his entering/ "Well hast thou done".'

After this great event, the rest of the decade of the 1980s might almost have seemed an anti-climax. But the following year, 1982, saw the visit of Pope John Paul II to Britain, an event in which the Holy Ghost parish, like all Catholic communities in the country, became deeply involved. Crowds gathered in the streets as the Pope went through London on his way to be greeted by the Queen at Buckingham Palace, and there were massive staged events at which he celebrated Mass and addressed the crowds. He visited St George's Cathedral, Southwark, for a Blessing of the Sick, an event for which people were brought on stretchers and gathered in the Cathedral beneath specially-made banners. The whole of the papal visit was widely televised. No longer were Catholics a fringe group on the margins of British life.

Up to the present

During the 1980s, the whole Church gradually emerged from the post-Vatican II confusion into a new era which saw the publication of a long-awaited Catechism restating the unchanging truths of the Faith in a clear way and tackling new issues that had not been mentioned in the previous Catechism published to mark the Council of Trent some 400 years earlier – divorce, contraception, homosexual activity, in-vitro fertilisation, euthanasia. These issues were also among those that deeply concerned Catholics and other Christians who viewed with anxiety the increasing evidence of social disintegration as laws protecting family life and marriage were abandoned, and hedonistic values celebrated in the mass media and through legislation.

In Balham, as elsewhere, local Catholics took the initiative in forming groups opposing legalized abortion, and defending the integrity of marriage and the family. The 'pro-life' movement began to play a big part in Catholic life, as volunteers went into schools to teach young people the vital need to cherish life from conception until natural death.

Ecumenism, which had seemed to open new doors for Christian action in the 1970s, rather withered as the Anglican church, at least in its official pronouncements, failed to take a clear stand on these issues, although clear alliances between Catholics and those – notably evangelical Christians – who wanted to speak up were forged and formed the basis of shared action in meetings, pamphlets, statements at General Elections, etc.

Debates continued about religious education in Catholic schools – nationwide the number of young people who stopped attending Mass while still in their teens caused continuing concern. Sad comparisons were drawn with earlier years, where a thriving Catholic community had weathered the storms of two World Wars without any apparent loss of confidence. There was also a continuing realization that Catholics could not but be influenced by the general trends of society: all sorts of things, from styles of dress to the widespread availability of pornography, simply affected everyone.

During the early 1990s, a major part of Balham's parish life took place not at Holy Ghost church but at the extra Mass centre established by Fr Bennett in Nightingale Lane – the chapel of St Oliver Plunket. This began as a response to the needs of elderly people and others who found it difficult to reach Nightingale Square, but gradually acquired a life of its own, with many young families attending a 10 a.m. Sunday Mass there.

In 1996, Fr Bennett retired, to be replaced as parish priest by Father Stephen Langridge. Ordained in 1989, Fr Stephen had been curate at a nearby local parish, St Bede's in Clapham Park, and at St Francis, Maidstone. He inherited a united parish and busy school, active Catholic organizations and a parish tradition now stretching back over a century.

The parish newsletter for the first months following his arrival reveal much activity. There was a party to bid farewell to the parish deacon, Geoffrey Smith, who was leaving for further studies in Rome preparatory to ordination as a priest. Various Nigerian priests came to stay, and were particularly useful in serving the needs of the substantial numbers of Nigerian Catholics in the parish, sometimes saying Mass in the Igbo language. The Plunkett Club – the parish's social club – continued to thrive and was open on Saturday evenings. A series of talks on Confession was given by a visiting speaker, Fr Timothy Finigan.

In 1997 Bishop Howard Tripp, auxiliary Bishop in Southwark, came for a special Mass to mark the parish centenary. Father Bennett was invited back to join the celebrations, together with various other priests who had worked as curates over the years. There was a centenary exhibition of photographs at the entrance to the church – including some pictures now featured in this book.

St Oliver Plunkett continued to feature in parish life – a group called 'The Companions of St Oliver Plunkett' ran an annual Race Night to raise funds to enable handicapped children to go to Lourdes. The St Oliver chapel in Nightingale Lane continued to function, but after a survey of people's Mass attendance needs, only a Saturday evening Mass was held there – mostly for older people – and the main Family Mass was moved to Holy Ghost church. In the Spring of 1997 a major clear-out of the church's crypt took place, with much accumulated rubbish from over the years being cleared away, and a Children's Liturgy was established for the smallest children (under 7s) who were taught simple doctrine and Scripture lessons, with handcraft and colouring work which was later taken up and presented at the Offertory of the Mass.

A forthright message was struck at the General Election of 1997. The local Member of Parliament, Tom Cox, a Catholic, told a meeting of Catholics that he would seek to abolish experimentation on human embryos – but the parish newsletter pointed out that he had on every possible occasion in Parliament voted in favour of such experiments and against any amending legislation which might possibly be considered pro-life. 'Please note, in publishing Mr Cox's record, we are not making a party political point,' the newsletter noted, 'simply pointing out an apparent and important inconsistency between what a sitting MP has done and what he claims he will do. We have a right to know how our MPs vote.'

Every year, as for the past hundred years, children in the parish made their First Communion. In 1997, the parish priest felt it important to point out that a primary requirement for this was regular attendance at Mass: 'Reception of Holy Communion is a fuller participation in the Mass. You cannot participate in something **more** fully unless you are already participating in it **less** fully!'

In June of that year, there was serious flooding following a sudden rainstorm. Volunteers took five hours to mop up the central aisle, front of the Lady Chapel, and the whole crypt area. It was also clear that the presbytery needed repairs – in the following spring major work was done to prevent further damage to the house from subsidence. Cracks in the walls had meant that kitchen utensils and items kept in wall cupboards were continually showered with dust. During 1997 work was also done on the house now known as Visitation House, to make it more suitable for parish use. The top floor was refurbished as a flat, bringing in much-needed rental income for the parish. The ground floor was made more suitable for formation activities with adults.

The autumn of 1997 saw the final abandonment of the St Oliver chapel as a parish Mass centre. The Catholic College next door needed it for its own purposes, and Masses were first temporarily suspended and then stopped altogether. However, the building, with its fine mosaic on the outside wall, remains as a reminder of the local devotion to St Oliver which flourished under the enthusiasm of Fr Bennett. The name is also commemorated in a new independent preparatory school, Oliver House, which opened in September 2004 as an initiative by parents, following the success of a similar school in Purley.

The summer of 1998 saw a revival of the tradition of the parish Corpus Christi procession. There were 52 First Communion children, and the canopy over the Blessed Sacrament was carried by members of the Knights and Ladies of Marshall, a Ghanain group analogous to the Knights of St Columba. The procession went right round Nightingale Square and ended with Benediction in the church.

Holy Ghost School, which had marked its own centenary in September 1997 with various celebrations and the gift of a special icon from the parish, blessed by Bishop Tripp, said farewell in 1998 to its headmaster Mr Hickey who retired after twelve years' dedicated service. Mrs Anne de Silva took over as acting head and Miss Susan

59

Lawless was appointed as the new head the following year, being presented with a Bible at a special welcome Mass. The following year would see a major refurbishment of the school with a new entrance hall and four new classrooms. The parish newsletter had commented that for some years the school had been functioning 'in accommodation designed largely for the late 19th century'. Now the combined efforts of Mrs de Silva and Miss Lawless had resulted in a fine new lobby, blending well with the church on one side and Visitation House on the other. The school was thriving and popular. There were many young families in the parish, and the district gloried in its nickname of 'Nappy Valley'. In 1998 there were 69 baptisms, rising to 89 in 2003. The parish newsletter regularly reminded parents about teaching their children how to participate at Mass: making the Sign of the Cross with holy water on entering the church, genuflecting, remaining quiet and talking only in a whisper, learning to recognize the Consecration and being encouraged to pray and adore.

A new curate, Father Dominic Allain, arrived in the summer of 1999. He had been a regular columnist on the *Catholic Times* newspaper as a seminarian studying in Rome. In early 2000 he gave a series of talks about the Mass. This was followed later in the year by a Parish Mission led by a team of young people from America. He remained at the parish until January 2001, when he was posted to St Joseph's, Bromley, and was replaced by Father Peter Gee.

Mass attendance figures at Balham have climbed steadily in recent years – from 680 in 1996 to more than 1,100 in 2004 – and are still climbing. There are many young families – the age profile of the parish shows the average age of Mass attenders to be 27!

As this account of the parish history goes to press, it is fascinating to look back and explore the interwoven lives of the many people who have belonged to Holy Ghost parish over the years: the young men who went from here to serve in two World Wars, the priests celebrating Mass and bringing the Sacraments to so many people, the hundreds of volunteers running everything from parish bazaars and whist drives to catechism classes and youth groups. It is also right to take a good look at the parish today.

It's an optimistic scene. For the eighth consecutive year, Holy Ghost church has bucked the national trend, and enjoyed a steady and substantial increase in attendance at Mass. Over eighty children a year are baptized and there are large numbers for First Confession and First Communion. There is a strong programme of adult education and formation, in partnership with the Maryvale Institute. Confessions are heard daily. There is an emphasis on communicating Catholic doctrine and the fullness of the Faith and its moral teachings. The music at the church, under the direction of Jeremy de Satgé, thrives with a choir singing in both Latin and English. In addition to the parish priest and his assistant, there is a parish sister, Sr Chiara Hatton Hall, based now in the flat at Visitation House. Recent work on the church has involved a new gold tabernacle, worked with designs depicting the Annunciation and the Holy Trinity, and replacing the old tabernacle which had become damp and rusted. There has also been much work to the sacristy including the installation of specially strengthened doors with automatic locking – a precaution against walk-in thieves. The introduction of confessions during Sunday Mass has seen an enormous increase in the use of this important sacrament, especially among young adults.

The church is bright and the marble floor of the sanctuary gleams. Subtle lighting focuses attention on the altar and the real presence in the golden tabernacle. At the entrance to the church, a neat but crowded noticeboard testifies to a wide range of activities, ranging from Mornings of Recollection to seasonal events such as Christmas carol services and the Good Friday walk of witness (an ecumènical event involving other local Christian groups).

Day by day, people drop in quietly to pray. As you enter the church, there are books to encourage and help children to learn about the Faith. The confessionals stand in the rear of the side-chapel (once the convent chapel) and are in frequent use. Statues – of St Thérèse and of the Sacred Heart – and a fine set of Stations of the Cross attract the eye.

On Sundays, the church is packed and people linger to talk to the parish priest and to one another. Balham is now always a place of roaring traffic, although Nightingale Square itself remains a pleasant residential square, and the church still has its 'village' feel.

It would be impossible to mention everyone who contributes to the life and work of Holy Ghost parish today – just as, inevitably, there have been many crucial names missed out in this parish history. A current 'who's who' of the parish lists, in addition to the clergy, Sister Chiara, and Jeremy de Satgé the music director, two organists, Daniel Fisher and Simon Perry, the housekeeper Jean Flynn, the sacristan Michael Cleveland-Peck, youth worker Natalie Ritchie, RCIA co-ordinator Janet Fyffe, parish secretary Valerie Slezak and chairman of the finance committee Denis Cross. This is a little community that has loved and served God in a London square for over a hundred years. The parish today is a testament to the sacrifices, generosity and faith of those who have gone before. The message of a parish history, such as this one, is that God stays with his people and the truths of the Faith are taught afresh to each new generation.

In Nightingale Square, the children's chatter as they pour out of school at the end of another day can be heard by the parish historian sifting through papers in the crypt beneath the sacristy. The children leave in cars that will take them home to pizza and computer games and TV, in a Britain where a dominant feature on the religious scene is the rise of Islam and where Catholics now form the largest single group of churchgoers in a Christianity which often feels under siege. The generation of Catholics now growing up faces great challenges. Courage will be needed to maintain the Faith and live its moral teachings.

In the quiet of the church the sanctuary lamp burns steadily as it always has, and a small but steady trickle of people come in to pray. The visitor who comes here finds peace and tranquillity, but not loneliness. The church in Nightingale Square is fulfilling the purpose for which it was built, in a very different England and an almost rural Balham, over a hundred years ago.

Printed in the United Kingdom
by Lightning Source UK Ltd.
105211UKS00001B/181-510